Praise for *Sick*

"Playwright Erik Patterson admits to personal hypochondria in the program notes for this resplendently twisted effort—yet another in his string of hilariously wicked and glaringly contemporary plays gloriously sending up the communal sickness that affects us all as our country becomes progressively more immune to wellness. CRITICS PICK."
—Travis Michael Holder, *Backstage*

"The two-character scenes that dominate the piece showcase Erik Patterson's edgy and hilarious play."
—Mayank Keshaviah, *LA Weekly*

"When it comes to walking the fine line between humor and misery, Erik Patterson is an experienced high-wire artist. Patterson's new play, *Sick*, is an incisive treatment of hypochondria and addiction that can be blisteringly funny... Subplots abound, and Patterson makes some sweetly salient points about the role of faith in the recovery process, as the people in Pamela's orbit struggle with their own burdensome brain chemistry."
—Kathleen Foley, *Los Angeles Times*

"Modern society at its best and most neurotic is the theme here in playwright Erik Patterson's smashing new play *Sick*."
—*Entertainment Today*

"Funny, personal, brutal at times, and profound... *Sick* packs a pretty enormous punch, and gives you a lot to think about and talk about afterwards."
—Sheila O'Malley, *The Sheila Variations*

Sick

Plays by Erik Patterson

Tonseisha

Yellow Flesh / Alabaster Rose

Red Light, Green Light

He Asked For It

Sick

I Wanna Hold Your Hand

One of the Nice Ones

Handjob

Books by Erik Patterson

Pop Prompts: 200 Writing Prompts Inspired by Popular Music

Pop Prompts For Swifties: 99 Writing Prompts

Sick

by Erik Patterson

Camden High Street Books
2023

Sick is copyright © 2023 by Erik Patterson

Sick is published by Camden High Street Books

All rights reserved. Except for brief passages quoted in newspaper, magazine, radio or television reviews, no part of this book may be reproduced in any form or by any means, electronic or mechanical, including photocopying or recording, or by an information storage and retrieval system, without permission in writing from the publisher.

Professionals and amateurs are hereby warned that this material, being fully protected under the Copyright Laws of the United States of America and all other countries of the Berne and Universal Copyright Conventions, is subject to a royalty. All rights, including but not limited to, professional, amateur, recording, motion picture, recitation, lecturing, public reading, radio and television broadcasting, and the rights of translation into foreign languages, are expressly reserved. Particular emphasis is placed on the question of readings and all uses of this book by educational institutions, permission for which must be secured from the publisher: camdenhighstreetbooks@gmail.com.

Performance Licensing and Royalty Payments. Amateur and professional performance rights to this Play are strictly reserved. No amateur or professional production groups or individuals may perform this Play without obtaining advance written permission. Required royalty fees must be paid every time the Play is performed before any audience, whether or not it is presented for profit and whether or not admission is charged. All licensing requests and inquiries concerning amateur and professional performance rights should be addressed to the author at erik@erikpatterson.org.

Print ISBN: 978-1-7379853-5-8 (Paperback)
eBook ISBN: 979-8-9878016-6-6

Library of Congress Control Number: 2023902516

First Paperback Edition, March 2023

Copy editing by Sherry Angel
Cover image by Bethany Beck on Unsplash

Printed in the United States of America
Los Angeles, CA
www.erikpatterson.org

For Diane.

PRODUCTION HISTORY

Sick had its world premiere at Playwrights' Arena (Jon Lawrence Rivera, Artistic Director) in Los Angeles on April 17, 2010. It was directed by Diane Rodriguez. The scenic and costume design was by Sandra Burns, the lighting design was by Adam Blumenthal, the sound design was by Dennis Yen, the casting director was Raul Clayton Staggs, the production stage managers were Pat Loeb and Caitlin Reinhart, the rehearsal stage manager was Crystal Munson, and it was produced by Diane Levine. The cast was:

PAMELA	Vanessa Martin
DAVID	Ramon de Ocampo
MICHAEL	Quinton Lopez
	Luca Oriel
BROWN	Brendan O'Malley
GARY	Johnny Giacalone
CARLA	Diarra Kilpatrick
	Regan Metoyer (alternate)
JEANNIE	Anita Dashiel

SETTING

Any city. The early 2000s.

CHARACTERS

PAMELA, a twenty-eight-year-old hypochondriac.

DAVID, her husband.

MICHAEL, their ten-year-old son.

BROWN, his doctor. Handsome, charming.

GARY, Pamela's brother.

CARLA, his wife.

JEANNIE, an addict, a sales clerk.

NOTES

There are many locations. We should move from one location to the next quickly, fluidly. There should be no intermission.

SCENE ONE

Outside an apartment building.

PAMELA and DAVID sit on a bench. Their son, MICHAEL, is on the ground a few feet away. He's transfixed by GARY, a drunk man yelling at the building.

Gary looks like shit: black eye, bloody mouth, his shirt ripped at the neck. Pamela and David ignore his antics.

PAMELA: I think I'm dying, David.
GARY: Fuck you!
PAMELA: I don't want to be a waitress anymore.
GARY: You motherfucking...fucker!
PAMELA: The restaurant's giving me cancer.
GARY: You fucking...fucking...FUCKER!
PAMELA: I hate it so much. Do you know how long I've been there?
    I've been, oh my god, I've been there for ten years.
GARY: Why do you have to be such a fucker?!?
PAMELA: I wish I could start over. What should I do, David?
DAVID: You could find another job.
PAMELA: But who would hire me? I can't *do* anything.
DAVID: We've talked about this. Take a class. Learn something.

PAMELA: That's good. I could take a class.

GARY: You...fucking—fuck!

PAMELA: But when am I gonna find the time to take a class?

DAVID: I don't know, Pamela.

PAMELA: I don't have any time.

DAVID: Then don't take a class.

GARY: You...stupid, fucking—fuck!

DAVID: Don't quit the restaurant. Don't do anything.

GARY: If you think I'm gonna fucking leave, then just—

He throws his shoe.

...You're a fucker!

DAVID: Just keep complaining. Since you do it so well.

PAMELA (*genuinely hurt*): Sorry...My day kinda sucked, that's all.

GARY: A fucking fucker!

PAMELA: There was this guy who sent his food back twice.

GARY: A fucking fuck-face fuckerrrr!

PAMELA: And this big party that tipped really bad.

GARY: I'm not leaving! I'm staying right here!

PAMELA: And then I had this really weird poop.

David can tell she wants him to ask about her poop...but he decides not to.

DAVID: That sucks. I'm sorry to hear you had such a bad day.

PAMELA: Yeah, it totally sucked.

DAVID: *My day* didn't suck.

PAMELA: It didn't?

DAVID: No...You gonna ask me about it?

PAMELA: I'm distracted. Sorry. How was your day?

DAVID: Fine. I left work early to go to Michael's game.

PAMELA: Oh no...I was wondering how he got so dirty.

DAVID: He had a game.

PAMELA: Right...How'd he play?

DAVID: He's getting better.

PAMELA: Did he score a goal?

DAVID: He hit a double.

PAMELA: So you think he'll play football when he grows up?

DAVID: He doesn't play football. He plays baseball.

PAMELA: You know I get all those ball games confused.

DAVID: They're completely different.

PAMELA: I said the wrong word, okay? It's not a big deal.

DAVID: Pam, it is a big deal. It's what our son does. He plays baseball. He had a game today. And you weren't there.

PAMELA: Can we talk about my poop?

DAVID: *Your poop.*

PAMELA: It was really weird.

DAVID: Weird how?

PAMELA: I don't know. Just different.

DAVID: How do you know it was different?

PAMELA: Because I know my poop. I know when it's normal. And I know when it's not. Today it was weird. I think it's because of the restaurant. You're giving me that look.

DAVID: I thought we weren't gonna do this anymore.

PAMELA: Do what?

DAVID: I can't do this. I thought we were over this.

PAMELA: Over what?

DAVID: Fine. Tell me why your job is making your poop weird.

GARY: I'm still here, you know!

PAMELA: Never mind, you're mad at me now.

GARY: And I'm not your fucking tool!

DAVID: No, you wanna talk about poop, let's talk about poop.

GARY: 'Cause I'm not fucked up!

PAMELA: Not if you're gonna be like that.

GARY: You are. You're fucked up!

DAVID: What do you want me to say? I'm listening. Talk.

GARY: Fucked up on coke, you fucking cokehead!

PAMELA: People are mean at the restaurant.

DAVID: They're mean?

GARY: *My ass* you're clean now—if so you'll be fucked up again!

PAMELA: You know how people get. When they're hungry, they get mean.

GARY: I mean, Jesus!

PAMELA: And they take their frustration and hunger out on me.

GARY: No—fuck Jesus!

PAMELA: And then I get mad. But I can't let them know I'm mad because I need their tips. So I smile. And my anger builds...

GARY: Jesus didn't die for my sins, not for fuckin' my sins!

PAMELA: But I suppress it. And when I pretend I'm not angry...

GARY: It's fucked up to say that, Jesus lover!

PAMELA: ...I think I tighten my anus. A lot.

GARY: You should be loving Gary...fuck Jesus...all over my ass...and shit, I mean FUCK! I'm your fucking husband!

PAMELA: And that must do something to my body, right?

GARY: Be my fucking wife!

PAMELA: It must be doing something.

GARY (*almost to himself, defeated*): Fucking woman-ass shit...getting all up in her...God...and fucking shit...and fuck.

PAMELA: Then I had this weird poop today and it made me realize that maybe all of that anger is manifesting itself in my bowels.

DAVID: Your poop was that weird?

PAMELA: You should've seen it David. It wasn't just weird poop. It was worse than that. It was angry poop.

DAVID: Then you should quit your job. Find something else.

PAMELA: I don't know. I'm hungry. What are we gonna do for dinner?

DAVID: We should get something. Take-out.

PAMELA: Give him a few more minutes. Then we'll go.

Gary starts punching the building.

DAVID: Michael?

    Michael, are you hungry?

    Mike.

MICHAEL: What?

DAVID: Are you hungry?

MICHAEL: Yeah.

DAVID: What do you want?

MICHAEL: I don't know.

DAVID: McDonald's?

MICHAEL: Yeah.

DAVID: Okay. You think you can wait a couple more minutes?

GARY: If you don't let me in right this fucking second you can eat shit and fucking die you fucking bitch!

    One final attempt:

I LOVE YOU!

    He lies on the ground for a moment, motionless.

MICHAEL: Mom, I think he's done.

PAMELA: Gary, are you done?

GARY (*to Pamela*): Fuck you.

PAMELA: Just tell me if you're done. Are you done, Gary?

GARY: No.

PAMELA: I want to go home. Let's go home.

GARY: Leave me the fuck alone.

PAMELA: I'm tired and I'm hungry.

GARY: So?

PAMELA: So come on, Gary. Carla's not gonna let you back in. Tell her to fuck off one more time and then let's go home.

GARY: I don't have a home anymore.

PAMELA: You're coming home with us.

Gary doesn't move.

Help me, David.

DAVID: Gary, your sister has a headache, let's go.

You wanna go to McDonald's, Gary?

Are you hungry, Gary?

GARY: No.

DAVID: It's just past seven-thirty. When was the last time you ate?

GARY: I don't know.

DAVID: Come with us. We'll feed you, we'll wash your face.

GARY: I don't want to wash my face.

DAVID: You'll feel better.

He touches Gary's bruised face. With compassion...

Gary, you look terrible.

GARY: Shut up.

David helps Gary off the ground.

DAVID: Let's go home.
GARY: This is my home.
DAVID: I know, but are you hungry?
GARY: Yeah.
DAVID: Then let's get some McDonald's.
GARY: I hate McDonald's.
DAVID: Michael wants it.
GARY: You like McDonald's?
MICHAEL: Yeah.
GARY: Well I hate that crap. So would you do your Uncle Gary a favor and tell your folks you wanna eat at fucking Del Taco?

Lights shift.

SCENE TWO

Pamela and David's kitchen.

Gary sits, holding frozen peas up to his face. Pam cleans up, throwing away trash from McDonald's, etc.

GARY: Where'd my other shoe go?
PAMELA: You threw it at Carla's window.
GARY: I only have one shoe now. That's fucked up.
PAMELA: Are you sober?
GARY: Getting there.

Pam pours a glass of wine for Gary.

GARY: She's such a bitch, you know? She keeps saying this stuff about God, and I'm all: fuck, I haven't even had my coffee yet. It's just like, that kinda fucking shit warps you. Cause I think about it and then my stomach gets even more twisted because: what the fuck is wrong with a little drink? Or a little coke? If God didn't want us to do it, he wouldn't of invented it, it's just simple logic. So the real question is: why's she gotta go around and say I'm defective? That's what she's saying! And it makes me wanna hate her because fuck. And then some of the things she does...piss me off so bad.

PAMELA: Like what? What things will she do?

> *Gary finishes his wine. Pam refills it.*

GARY: You know, just...like, I don't know, it's not even that she'll do...one thing. Just...stuff.
Where's Michael?
PAMELA: David's putting him to bed.
GARY: It's early.
PAMELA: School night.
GARY: I was gonna see if he wanted to play a video game.
PAMELA: I'd say yes, but David'll say no.
GARY: Well, then, can I play a video game?
PAMELA: They're in Michael's room.
So, no. He's in bed.
GARY: I could move the video games to the living room...
PAMELA: Look, I'm gonna let you stay here. I'm gonna let you live here as long as you want. Until Carla invites you back home. Or until you get your own place. I won't ever pressure you to leave. You can think of this place as your own home, I swear.
GARY: Thanks, Pam.
PAMELA: But you gotta shut up when I tell you to shut up.

> *Beat.*

Just hang out with me.

GARY: No offense, I love you and shit, but I wish you were Carla.

PAMELA: I know. Sorry...

GARY: She's hated me before, but it was, like, 'cause she loved me so much. But the God stuff's new and I'm afraid He's gonna make her hate me for real this time. You think that could happen?

PAMELA: I don't know Gary. Sometimes people change. They just change.

GARY: I don't get why she hasn't called me. That's all I want—a phone call. Just one fucking phone call.

Pamela makes a "phone" shape with her hand, puts it up to her ear.

PAMELA: Ring, ring. Ring, ring.

GARY (*playing along*): Hello?

PAMELA (*putting on a deep voice*): Hello, Gary.

GARY: Is this supposed to be Carla?

PAMELA: No, Gary, this is God.

GARY: Shit.

PAMELA: I have a message for you.

GARY: What is it?

PAMELA: Something I've been meaning to tell you...

GARY: Yeah?

PAMELA: You stink. Seriously, it's so bad. Have you ever heard of deodorant? Is it possible to die of smelling someone because you're killing me. You should shower. Shower!

They get into a playful shoving match, like two kids.

After a few beats, they stop. Gary pours himself some wine.

PAMELA: Gary...? I need you to feel my left breast.

GARY: What?

PAMELA: What I said.

GARY: Why?

PAMELA: I think I have a lump.

GARY: I don't want to touch your boobs.

PAMELA: I'm freaking out, Gary.

GARY: Get David to do it.

PAMELA: I don't want him to know—

GARY: He's your husband.

PAMELA: —unless I know it's really something.

GARY: Pam, if you're worried—

PAMELA: I'm worried.

GARY: Then you should talk to David—

PAMELA: Just, stop, okay? Will you do it?

GARY: It's kinda weird.

PAMELA: It's medical.

GARY: It doesn't seem medical.

PAMELA: I don't want you to cop a feel, just tell me I have cancer.

GARY: You don't want me to tell you you have cancer.

PAMELA: I said, *if* I have cancer. I want you to tell me *if*.

GARY: That's not what you said.

PAMELA: It is.

GARY: Is not.

PAMELA: Is too. Look, I don't care what I said, it's what I meant.

GARY: You don't have cancer, Pam.

PAMELA: Everyone I know has cancer.

GARY: Who? Who do you know that has it? Specifically?

PAMELA: Mom had cancer.

GARY: Besides mom.

PAMELA: A lot of people, Gary.

GARY: Name three. Other than mom. Three other people.

PAMELA: Aunt Meg. She had it.

GARY: That's one.

PAMELA: David's sister...

GARY: That's two.

PAMELA: And me.

GARY: You can't say yourself.

PAMELA: Why not?

GARY: 'Cause you don't have it!

PAMELA: Just touch my boob. Touch it and tell me if you feel a lump.

Beat.

Gary feels for a lump.

GARY: It feels good. Well, not good, that's the wrong word, but it feels normal. Not that it's normal to feel your sister's boob, but the boob itself feels fine. Healthy. It feels...

He removes his hand.

Don't tell anyone I touched that, okay?

Beat.

Lights shift.

SCENE THREE

A church basement.

CARLA fixes herself a cup of coffee. She adds some sugar, some half-and-half. Then she pours it out into the trash.

JEANNIE approaches.

JEANNIE: I'm gonna have to tell on you.

CARLA: What do you mean?

JEANNIE: Wasting coffee like that.

CARLA: Oh, I—

JEANNIE: I'm kidding.

CARLA: Funny.

JEANNIE: Is it that bad?

CARLA: I don't know. I didn't try it.

JEANNIE: Coffee's coffee. I just need the caffeine. I'm Jeannie.

CARLA: Carla.

JEANNIE: So, was it good for you too? The meeting.

CARLA: It was great.

JEANNIE: You're a bad liar.

CARLA: Sometimes it's better to fake it. Isn't that what they say?

JEANNIE: "Fake it 'til you make it." That's what they say. So, what step are you on?

CARLA: Number six.

JEANNIE: You're "entirely ready to have God remove all of your defects of character?"

CARLA: Those are the exact words of the step.

JEANNIE: I know all twelve by heart. I find it helpful. Number six is a good one.

CARLA: I guess. It's hard.

JEANNIE: Look on the bright side: it's number six. You're halfway through the steps.

CARLA: Well, I'm skipping around a little.

JEANNIE: Skipping around?

CARLA: I haven't done four and five yet.

JEANNIE: You haven't made "a searching and fearless moral inventory of yourself?"

CARLA: Number four.

JEANNIE: And you haven't "admitted to God, yourself, and another human being the exact nature of your wrongs?"

CARLA: Number five. Wow, you really do have them memorized.

JEANNIE: I'm on number twelve.

CARLA: Congratulations.

JEANNIE: So you've only done one, two, three, and six?

CARLA: I thought six would help me get through four and five. But I don't know yet 'cause I only did it last night.

JEANNIE: Honey, you don't do the steps one time and then forget about them. You keep doing them for the rest of your life.

CARLA: I know, but number six is all about getting rid of your main defects of character, and that's always been my husband Gary. I've been ready for God to remove him for about two months. Ever since I started to get clean. But God didn't remove Gary. So I had to do it myself.

JEANNIE: How'd you do it?

CARLA: I beat him up. Not bad. Just enough. Then I threw him out and I called his sister to pick him up. And now he's gone.

JEANNIE: I don't think you should think of your "main defect of character" as another person. It's supposed to be something inside that you need to change.

CARLA: That's him, though. He's inside me...inside here.

JEANNIE: It takes time.

CARLA: The thing is, I love him. I really love him. But when he's fucked up, I want to be fucked up. I can't be around that.

JEANNIE: Then you did the right thing.

CARLA: I want to call him, though.

JEANNIE: Don't call him. You can't risk it.

CARLA: But it's hard. Not calling him is really fucking hard.

JEANNIE: That's 'cause you skipped step number four.

CARLA: What's number four again?

JEANNIE: "Be fearless. And don't call the bastard."

Lights shift.

SCENE FOUR

A few days later. A sterile white hospital room. Pamela sits on the edge of an examining table, with DR. BROWN.

PAMELA: Thank you so much for seeing me.

BROWN: Of course.

PAMELA: I know this is...

BROWN: It's—

PAMELA: It's highly...

BROWN: Unusual?

PAMELA: Yeah.

BROWN: Not as unusual as you'd think.

PAMELA: No?

BROWN: I get calls from parents all the time.

PAMELA: You do?

BROWN: Asking for my opinion.

PAMELA: Really?

BROWN: Sure. They like how I treat their kids. They want me to treat them too. I get it all the time.

PAMELA: And?

BROWN: I say no.

PAMELA: You just say no?

BROWN: Hey, when a woman like yourself calls me on the phone asking me to perform a breast exam, I tell her it's not my area of expertise—most of my patients don't have breasts.

PAMELA: What's that supposed to mean?

BROWN: They're children.

PAMELA: Of course. I'm sorry. I thought you were...making fun of my breasts. But let me get this straight: mothers call you all the time asking for your help but usually you say no, except here I am, you're seeing me. So what made you...?

BROWN: You sounded very upset on the phone.

PAMELA: I am. I'm freaking out. And I didn't know who else to call. My regular doctor wouldn't see me.

BROWN: Why not?

PAMELA: He's on vacation. That's why I called you.

BROWN: Shall we get this over with?

PAMELA: Should I lay down? There's isn't enough room. Where do you want me?

BROWN: You're fine right there. But I need you to open your blouse.

As he performs the exam:

How's Michael?

PAMELA: He's doing good.

BROWN: Is he still playing baseball?

PAMELA: Yeah.

BROWN: Does he still like dinosaurs? Last time I saw him he said he wanted to be a paleontologist.

Beat.

Pamela?

PAMELA: What?

BROWN: I asked if Michael still wanted to be a paleontologist.

PAMELA: Oh I got distracted. It's my head. On Monday I was the victim of biological terrorism and it gave me a really bad headache.

BROWN: Excuse me, what was that?

PAMELA: Bombshell, I know. But it's true. On Monday I was the victim of biological terrorism and blammo: my head won't stop throbbing. But don't worry, I'm not contagious—

BROWN: I'm not worried—

PAMELA: And I'm not crazy, I know it isn't going to kill me—

BROWN: Look, why don't we...

PAMELA: Yeah...? What?

BROWN: Why don't you tell me what happened? From the beginning.

PAMELA: This happened three days ago. I was standing on the street outside Michael's school. School wasn't out yet, but I don't like sitting in parked cars, so I was standing out on the sidewalk. Waiting to pick up Michael. Just standing there, minding my own business, when this man threw something at me.

BROWN: Did you see him?

PAMELA: No, he was in his car.

BROWN: But you're sure he threw it at you?

PAMELA: I don't know if he was throwing it at me specifically. But it landed at my feet, then he drove off. When I looked at the ground and saw this silver bag, I wasn't thinking: "This is biological terrorism." I wasn't thinking: "Someone's trying to kill me." NO, I was thinking: "Why would someone litter?" I was thinking: "I should pick that up." So I leaned down and then: it popped. In my face. And I was overwhelmed with this smell—this smell of, oh god—this rotten egg smell? That's when I realized I was an idiot. Because you don't just pick up strange objects like that anymore. Strange bags. It's too dangerous. You never know what something's gonna be. So then I got Michael. And we went home. That's when my headache started. But I know what I have. Have you ever heard of hydrogen sulfide poisoning? Hydrogen sulfide is this gas that smells like rotten egg. If you inhale too much of it, it'll kill you. Like, sniff, you're dead. But I'm here because, fortunately, I didn't inhale very much—just enough to get a nasty headache.

BROWN: Where'd you hear about hydrogen sulfide poisoning?

PAMELA: I looked up rotten egg smell on Google and a thousand pages on hydrogen sulfide came up.

BROWN: Someone threw a stink bomb at you.

PAMELA: Wait, what? What's that?

BROWN: It's a tiny little bomb that smells.

PAMELA: You're making fun of me.

BROWN: People don't go around with hydrogen sulfide. But if they did, and if they threw some at you, you'd have more than a headache: you'd be puking your guts out. But you're not puking your guts out because hydrogen sulfide poisoning is an extremely rare occurrence that mostly affects miners.

PAMELA: Kids?

BROWN: People who work in mine shafts.

PAMELA: Oh.

BROWN: People do, however, go around with stink bombs. Especially near elementary schools. And stink bombs smell like rotten egg. So...what do you think that guy threw at you?

PAMELA: A stink bomb?

BROWN: Yes.

And you can button up your blouse.

PAMELA: You're done? What did you find?

BROWN: You're fine.

PAMELA: Then what's this?

She presses a spot on her chest.

BROWN: That's your rib cage. Look, if it'll ease your mind, get a mammogram when your doctor gets back into town, but honestly, I wouldn't bother: you're too young to start getting—

PAMELA: I had my first mammogram last summer.

BROWN: Well, I find that unnecessary. I doubt you have cancer.

PAMELA: What kind of doctor are you? You "doubt" I have cancer?

BROWN: I'm certain. You're young. You're healthy.

You can smile.

It's good news.

PAMELA: It's a relief.

BROWN: Do you feel better now?

PAMELA: I do. Thank you, Dr. Brown.

BROWN: Wait. Before you go. Pick a hand.

He holds out two clenched fists. She points at one. He opens it, revealing...

PAMELA: A toy truck?

BROWN: Sorry, but we're all out of girl toys.

Lights shift.

SCENE FIVE

About a week later.

Michael sits at the kitchen table, playing with the toy truck. Gary serves up two bowls of Mac and Cheese.

GARY: Stop playing with that truck and eat.

MICHAEL: I'm not hungry.

GARY: Yeah, you are.

MICHAEL: No, I feel sick.

GARY: Because you didn't eat lunch.

MICHAEL: No.

GARY: I told you, you should've eaten lunch.

MICHAEL: I don't feel well.

GARY: Because you're hungry.

MICHAEL: I think I'm gonna throw up.

GARY: Shit, for real?

MICHAEL: I don't know, maybe.

GARY: Don't say that unless you're really gonna throw up.

MICHAEL: I am.

GARY: Now?

MICHAEL: No.

GARY: Well, don't. Just eat.

MICHAEL (*taking a bite*): This is gross.

GARY: It's good.

MICHAEL: I hate this.

GARY: You love it.

MICHAEL: No, I don't. I hate it.

GARY: Macaroni and cheese is, like, your favorite thing to eat. You used to beg me to make it for you, remember?

MICHAEL: That was when I was six.

GARY: So?

MICHAEL: So, I'm ten now. And now I don't like it.

GARY: Just eat it.

MICHAEL: If I throw up—

GARY: Don't throw up.

MICHAEL: But if I do it's gonna be your fault.

Gary grabs a pot from the cupboard.

GARY: Do it in here if you do it. And warn me so I don't have to watch. Now eat.

Michael picks at his food.

MICHAEL: When are mom and dad coming home?

GARY: Soon.

MICHAEL: But when?

GARY: I don't know, after you're in bed.

MICHAEL: Where are they?

GARY: The hospital.

MICHAEL: Again?

GARY: Yeah.

MICHAEL: Is mom gonna die?

GARY: Not today.

MICHAEL: But someday?

GARY: Of course.

MICHAEL: I feel sick.

GARY: For real this time? You're gonna throw up?

MICHAEL: No. It just hurts.

GARY: You're not faking?

MICHAEL: No.

GARY: What hurts?

Michael holds his stomach.

It's probably because you didn't eat anything today. What if I gave you Pepto-Bismol?

MICHAEL: It makes me throw up.

GARY: Okay, wait, let me think...Okay. I have an idea.

MICHAEL: What is it?

GARY: Only if you can keep a secret. Can you keep a secret?

MICHAEL: Yeah.

GARY: It's a big secret. You promise you can keep it?

MICHAEL: Yeah.

GARY: I could give you something that would make you feel one-hundred-percent better, but you'd have to super-for-real promise never to tell your mom or your dad.

MICHAEL: I promise.

GARY: How do I know you aren't lying? And remember: I'm your uncle, so you gotta give me your shit straight.

MICHAEL: I'm not a liar. I never lie.

GARY: For reals? Spit on it.

They spit in their palms, shake hands.

GARY: You're a good kid.

Gary takes a baggie out of his pocket and starts rolling a joint.

MICHAEL: What's that?

GARY: It's pot.

MICHAEL: What's pot?

GARY: You smoke it and then you feel better.

MICHAEL: Smoking kills.

GARY: That's true. That's good. But when they say "smoking kills," they're talking about cigarettes. Which kill, so you should never smoke them. But this isn't a cigarette.

MICHAEL: Then what is it?

GARY: It's a joint. It's good for you. It's like medicine.

MICHAEL: So why can't I tell mom and dad?

GARY: Because you're not supposed to take this medicine until you're older.

MICHAEL: Why not?

GARY: Because people are stupid.

MICHAEL: But why?

GARY: Look, do you want to feel better or not?

MICHAEL: Yeah.

GARY: Then stop asking me questions and trust me. I'm your uncle. I'm not gonna kill you.

He takes a hit.

You wanna pull the smoke all the way into your lungs, hold it, then let it out. Like you're taking a deep breath. Watch.

Gary demonstrates.

See. Now, you're a little guy, so you're probably gonna cough the first time you try it, but that's okay.

He hands Michael the joint.

Don't press your lips onto the joint too tight. And don't get it wet with your mouth.

> *Michael inhales, immediately starts coughing.*

I told you, you're gonna cough the first time.

MICHAEL: It burns.

GARY: That's okay, the first time you do it, it's gonna burn the back of your throat. I shoulda told you that. But the burn is good. Now try again. And try to hold it in longer this time. You wanna hold it in as long as you can.

> *Michael inhales. He holds it in for about three seconds, then starts coughing again.*

You wanna hold it in longer than that, but that's a good start. Okay, puff, puff, give. My turn.

> *Michael hands the joint to Gary, who takes another hit.*

MICHAEL: My stomach still hurts.

GARY: Don't worry, it might take a few hits. This is your first time, so you might not feel better til you smoke a lot of it.

> *Gary takes another hit.*

Puff, puff, give.

> *He passes to Michael.*

Remember, you wanna hold it in as long as you can. You really wanna intake it.

> *Michael takes a hit, holds it in, and exhales. No coughing.*

Nice job. That was good.
MICHAEL: Really?
GARY: Yeah. Now do it again.

> *Michael takes another effortless hit.*

Look at you, you're a little pro all of a sudden. You starting to feel better yet?
MICHAEL: I think so.
GARY: Okay, now it's my turn again. Puff, puff, give, remember?

> *Michael hands the joint to Gary, who takes another hit.*

MICHAEL: Hey, Uncle Gary?
GARY: Yeah.

MICHAEL: Did Aunt Carla really beat you up?

GARY: Where'd you hear that?

MICHAEL: I heard mom and dad talking about it.

GARY: That's so fucked up.

Gary takes another hit.

MICHAEL: Did she beat you up?

GARY: Yeah.

MICHAEL: That's really weird.

GARY: Don't tell anyone, okay?

MICHAEL: I won't.

GARY: Thanks.

MICHAEL: I can't believe a girl beat you up.

GARY: I know.

MICHAEL: It's so weird.

GARY: It happens, though. Nobody's perfect.

MICHAEL: Hey, Uncle Gary—

GARY: Yeah?

MICHAEL: My turn. Puff, puff, give, remember?

Gary hands the joint to Michael, who takes a hit.

There's this girl at my school, Amanda. We call her Man-duh 'cause she's a foot taller than everyone and she looks like a man.

GARY: You guys are funny.

MICHAEL: This one time she beat up my friend Chad because he was making fun of her. And now everyone makes fun of Chad because he got beat up by a girl.

GARY: That sucks.

MICHAEL: I was making fun of her too, but she only hit me once. She didn't beat me up.

GARY: Good thing.

MICHAEL: I forget why we're talking about Man-duh.

GARY: Because your Aunt Carla beat me up.

MICHAEL: That's really weird. I can't believe a girl beat you up.

GARY: Puff, puff, give.

Michael hands the now almost-finished joint to Gary.

I bet the reason Man-duh hit you is because she likes you.

MICHAEL: Really?

GARY: Probably.

MICHAEL: Well, I don't like her.

GARY: Maybe one day you will.

MICHAEL: Probably not.

GARY: Keep an open mind, you never know.

MICHAEL: So if Aunt Carla beat you up does that mean she likes you?

GARY: I hope so.

MICHAEL: Uncle Gary...? I feel better.

GARY: I knew it would help your stomach ache. Now eat your macaroni and cheese.

MICHAEL: That actually sounds good.

GARY: I told you—you like it.

MICHAEL: I don't like it, but I want it.

GARY: Funny. That's exactly how I feel about your Aunt Carla.

Lights shift.

SCENE SIX

A few weeks later.

A supermarket produce aisle. Carla enters, sizes up a few cantaloupes. David enters from the other end of the aisle.

DAVID: Carla—
CARLA: David—hi.

There's something awkward in the air.

DAVID: Hey.
CARLA: What are you doing here?
DAVID: Groceries.
CARLA: Of course. Me too.
DAVID: It's a grocery store.
CARLA: Right. I'm looking for a melon. I forget how you're supposed to tell when they're ripe.
DAVID: Let me—

David reaches for the melon in Carla's hand. Grazes Carla. She pulls away.

CARLA: Don't touch me.

DAVID: Sorry.

CARLA: This is a supermarket.

DAVID: Don't freak out. Jesus.

CARLA: And don't take the Lord's name in vain.

DAVID: What the fuck?

CARLA: David, your mouth.

DAVID: I was just saying hello.

CARLA: That's not how you say hello.

DAVID: Then how do you say it?

CARLA: "Hello."

DAVID: What's wrong with you? Why are you flipping out—

CARLA: With me? What's wrong with me? You walk up to me in the supermarket, you practically attack me, and then you have the gall to ask: what's wrong with me? To say I'm "flipping out?"

DAVID: Well, yeah.

CARLA: You can't just grab someone.

DAVID: I didn't grab you.

CARLA: You grabbed my hand.

DAVID: I was reaching for the fruit.

CARLA: Somebody might've seen.

DAVID: I was trying to help you—

CARLA: Keep your voice down—

DAVID: I'm not yelling.

CARLA: I'm never kissing you again, so stop harassing me.

DAVID: Whoa. Hold on. I'm sorry, but we need to talk. I've been waiting for your call.

CARLA: That's pathetic, David.

DAVID: No, don't judge me. I just happened to be at the supermarket, doing some shopping, and I just happened to see you standing over here. I thought maybe now we'd have a chance to talk. But I didn't grab you. I didn't do anything nasty. I didn't attack you. I just touched you. That's all. So back off.

CARLA: Sorry...

DAVID: Listen—I haven't been able to stop thinking about you since we kissed and maybe I am pathetic but I kinda like you, okay?

CARLA: No, not okay.

DAVID: What?

CARLA: You "kinda like me?"

DAVID: Maybe I do.

CARLA: This isn't high school, David.

DAVID: We kissed one time. I don't know what's wrong with that.

CARLA: We're married! To other people. That's what's wrong with it! That's why I didn't call you. If I want to be sober, to really be sober, then I have to get rid of the bad influences in my life. I have to clean house. That's why I got rid of Gary. And you, David...you. You're a great guy, but—

DAVID: Am I?

CARLA: Yes, David—you are. But the only man I want in my life right now is God. No other men. I'm working on me right now.

DAVID: Okay, I hear you, but...

CARLA: But what, David?

DAVID: But now that you're not with Gary...I think I could love you.

CARLA: Did you hear anything I just said?

DAVID: Yeah.

CARLA: Then are you insane? Because you sound insane. Don't you love your wife?

DAVID: I do, but...we haven't made love in years.

CARLA (*too much info*): Whoa...

DAVID: It's true.

CARLA: That's none of my business.

DAVID: We sleep together, next to each other. And that's nice, I guess. It's nice to hold someone. But it's been years since we've had sex.

CARLA: David, if you want to talk about these things, you should be in therapy. You should talk to a therapist.

DAVID: No, listen: when I met Pamela, she seemed so vulnerable. She was so young and needy and sick, and that seemed like an attractive quality back then. She really needed me. And for a while, Pamela and I had passion—I mean, we had a real animal thing at first. She was...hot.

CARLA: Why are you telling me this?

DAVID: I need you to know how I got to this place—

CARLA: I don't want to know—

DAVID: So, then Pamela and I stopped making love because—

CARLA: Really, David, stop—

DAVID: No, no, I need to say this. Pamela and I stopped making love because she was afraid I was gonna hurt her, she was afraid of my body, of her body, of—by then she was just afraid of...everything. And so I started taking care of her. And I've been taking care of her for so long now that I almost feel like she's one of my kids, like I have two kids: Michael's the good one and Pamela...she's the difficult one. It's okay, though, because I'm a good dad and I can be there when she needs me. It's just that... I'm needy too, now...

CARLA: David...please...just stop...

DAVID: And you...when you and I kissed—it was like, for a second, I wasn't somebody's father: I was a man again.

CARLA: When I said talk to a therapist, I didn't mean me...

DAVID: I love Pam, but I don't want to kiss her anymore. But you...I would definitely like to kiss you again. To make love to you. Does that sound corny? Or is there some part of you that understands what I'm saying? That feels the same way?

CARLA: David, I don't know how to say this without hurting you—

DAVID: Say it. Hurt me.

CARLA: The kiss we had didn't mean anything to me. I was high. I don't even really remember it.

David's cell phone beeps.

DAVID: It's a text. It says "nine-one-one."

CARLA: From Pamela? That's all it says? It's an emergency?

DAVID: I doubt it.

CARLA: But you should go.

DAVID: Probably.

CARLA: ...you're not moving.

DAVID: I love her too.

CARLA: I know you do.

DAVID: I don't want to hurt her.

The phone beeps again.

CARLA: You should go. You should see what she wants.

DAVID: I will. I'll go. But one last thing...You want a melon that's soft, but not too soft. That's how you find one that's ripe.

CARLA: I'm sorry, David.

DAVID: Yeah, okay.

David exits.

Lights shift.

SCENE SEVEN

Later that night.

A hospital waiting room. David and Gary sit, waiting.

GARY: This is so fucked up. I can't believe this. It's just so fucked up.

DAVID: You said that.

GARY: But I can't believe it. I really can't.

DAVID: I know.

GARY: It's just so fucked up, you know?

DAVID: Gary, shut up.

GARY: I'm sorry.

DAVID: I need some headspace.

GARY: No, it's cool. I'll shut up, it's totally cool.

DAVID: Cool.

GARY: It's like, God has this really big dick and he's fucking all of our asses with it, you know? It's just like, so, so...

DAVID: So fucked up?

GARY: Yeah.

DAVID: Gary, listen, I can tell you're having a hard time giving me the headspace that I need.

GARY: I guess I am.

DAVID: Okay, then here's the deal: you don't have to shut up...but could you stop being so negative?

GARY: Oh—

DAVID: It's just—

GARY: Yeah—

DAVID: Really—

GARY: Sure—

DAVID: Not what I want to hear right now.

GARY: Whatever you want...So how about some good news?

DAVID: Good news would be good.

GARY: I decided I'm gonna win Carla back.

DAVID: How're you gonna do that?

GARY: She wants me to go to AA and believe in God and all that shit, but it's stupid. I'm just gonna change. I mean people change, sometimes. And she's gotta see that I'm trying. I wanna be better. You know I can be better, don't you, David?

DAVID: Sure, Gary.

GARY: Sometimes you just gotta believe.

Beat.

DAVID: You wanna hear something crazy? This is where Pam and I met. This hospital. Downstairs. The emergency waiting room.

GARY: No way.

DAVID: I slammed a door on my hand. I broke it. It was a stupid accident. I was waiting for them to call my name. Pamela sat next to me. She was dying. That's what she said at least.

GARY: And you believed her?

DAVID: I didn't know her yet, so why wouldn't I believe her?

GARY: Maybe because she's crazy?

DAVID (*playful*): Shut up—

GARY: But it's true!

DAVID: That's my wife you're talking about.

GARY: Your crazy wife.

DAVID: I can still picture the look on her face when she told me. She was so certain. So serious. And I remember thinking: I could fall in love with this girl. This girl could be "the one." But she's dying. It was all so tragically romantic.

GARY: What was she dying of that time? Cancer?

DAVID: Lung cancer.

GARY: It was winter? She had a cold?

DAVID: Yeah.

GARY: I can't believe you bought that shit.

DAVID: We were in the hospital. It made sense.

GARY: She can be really convincing.

DAVID: Yeah.

GARY: If you don't know her.

DAVID: You're right, though.

GARY: About what?

DAVID: This. It's so fucked up. I mean, since Pamela and I met, I don't know how many times we've been here, in this hospital. Waiting to find out she's okay, that it's all in her head. Just waiting. And here we are, waiting, again. But this time: it's real. Something's wrong. Something's really wrong. This time it's not in her head. And I don't know what to do. I mean, I can handle false alarms, I can handle panic attacks, I can handle tests that don't say anything. But all of a sudden they do say something? What the fuck am I supposed to do with that? When it's not in her head anymore? This place, I'm not used to being afraid here. And now they're telling me to be afraid? Because this sickness is real? I don't know what to do with that. I don't.

Pamela appears at the doorway.

Well?
PAMELA: We can take him home—
DAVID: That's good.
PAMELA: But we have to bring him back tomorrow for another biopsy.
DAVID: And then what?
PAMELA: I don't know.

Lights shift.

SCENE EIGHT

A couple of days later. A hospital room.

Michael sits, alone, in a hospital bed, wearing a hospital gown.

Dr. Brown stands in the doorway.

BROWN: Can I come in?
MICHAEL: Hi, Dr. Brown.

Dr. Brown enters.

MICHAEL: What are you doing here?
BROWN: I thought I'd check on you.
MICHAEL: Really?
BROWN: How are you doing?
MICHAEL: Fine.
BROWN: You're here all alone?
MICHAEL: Dad's at work. Mom had to go to the bathroom.
BROWN: So she'll be back in a minute?
MICHAEL: She doesn't use public bathrooms. She went home.
BROWN: I wanted to see you in case you had any questions.
MICHAEL: Okay.
BROWN: Do you like Dr. Carlson?

MICHAEL: He's fine.

BROWN: He's a good oncologist.

MICHAEL: What's that?

BROWN: It's a fancy name for the kind of doctor he is. He's gonna make you better. Okay?

MICHAEL: Okay. Dr. Brown? I have a question. What's a spinal tap?

BROWN: No one's told you?

MICHAEL: They told me I'm gonna get one. That's all. But I don't know what it is.

BROWN: No one's had this conversation with you? Dr. Carlson, your mom, your dad...no one?

Michael shakes his head, no.

It's a test they do to make sure the cancer hasn't spread throughout your body.

MICHAEL: Really? Oh. Okay.

BROWN: I'm sorry nobody—

MICHAEL: It's okay. I have another question.

BROWN: Ask me anything you want.

MICHAEL: Do I have the same kind of cancer my mom has?

BROWN: Your mom doesn't have cancer.

MICHAEL: Yes she does.

BROWN: No, Michael, I'm certain she doesn't.

MICHAEL: She's my mom. I've known her my whole life. I know what she has. Ever since I was in the first grade. That's when I found out. She's prone to things like this.

BROWN: Michael...wow, I—.

Beat.

Are you worried about her?

Michael nods.

Well, listen. I'm a doctor. And I checked your mom out. And the thing she has? It's not cancer. You don't have to worry about her.

MICHAEL: I'm gonna die, right? That's what I heard Dr. Carlson say.

BROWN: He said that? He shouldn't have said that.

MICHAEL: Not exactly, but basically. He told my mom and dad. He told them to "be prepared." So...is it true? Am I?

BROWN: You still play baseball, right?

MICHAEL: Of course.

BROWN: Then think about it like this: it's the bottom of the sixth inning, and you're playing a really difficult team, and right now they're ahead by a couple of runs. But even though this other team might be really tough, it's only the bottom of the sixth, so you still have a few more innings, and if you play hard enough, you can beat 'em. You just gotta stay positive and bring in a few more runs.

MICHAEL: I think you're trying to make me feel better, Dr. Brown. But you know how much that sucks, right? It totally sucks.

BROWN: You need to have a positive attitude—

MICHAEL: But how am I supposed to beat this other team if I don't have anyone else on *my* team? That's, like, automatic forfeit.

BROWN: Look…you can call me anytime, okay Michael? Whenever you have any questions. You can always call me. Okay?

Michael nods. Tentative. Uncertain.

Lights shift.

SCENE NINE

Several days later.

The same street corner from before.

Gary stands on the corner, yelling up at Carla's window.

GARY: Carla!
  Carla, come on, I know you're in there!
  Come on, let me in!

Carla enters from behind Gary.

GARY: Carla! I'm not leaving until you let me in!
CARLA: Gary? What are you doing here?

He turns to see Carla.

GARY: I thought you were inside.
CARLA: No.
GARY: I was calling you.
CARLA: I have a phone.
GARY: You never pick up.
CARLA: I don't want to talk to you.

GARY: Don't be mean.

CARLA: It's the truth.

GARY: It's a mean truth.

CARLA: What are you doing here?

GARY: I want you to take me back—

CARLA: Gary—

GARY: Don't you think you could give me one more chance?

CARLA: No.

GARY: I have a proposal, about how I can be a better husband—

CARLA: I don't want to hear it.

GARY: Just listen!

CARLA: I can't take you back, Gary.

GARY: Hear me out.

CARLA: You shouldn't even be here right now.

GARY: But I still love you.

CARLA: You should've called.

GARY: I didn't want you to tell me not to come over.

CARLA: I already told you not to come over. Don't come over.

GARY: Be nice, Carla.

CARLA: Just go.

GARY: You're not even gonna listen to my proposal?

CARLA: Does it involve accepting a power greater than yourself? Does it involve turning your will over to that higher power? How about admitting you have a problem? Does it involve any of those things? Because I need all of those things, Gary. And I need to know that you're gonna stay clean.

GARY: The proposal involves some of those things, yeah.

CARLA: My answer's no, Gary.

GARY: That's bullshit.

CARLA: What's bullshit about it?

GARY: I wanna change for you. You won't let me?

CARLA: You say you're gonna change, but you never actually do it, Gary. If you go to AA, if you follow the steps, at least that gives me the proof you're actually trying.

GARY: No. No fucking way. AA makes people believe all that God shit and God made Michael sick. So God can fuck himself.

CARLA: Michael's sick?

GARY: Yeah, it's bad, so shut up about it, listen to my proposal...

CARLA: What's he sick with?

GARY: Cancer, okay?

CARLA: Oh my god, that's awful.

It's bad?

GARY: Yeah. So would you just...would you listen to my proposal?

CARLA: Fine.

GARY: You will?

CARLA: Whatever. Lay it on me.

GARY: Okay. So I decided...I'm gonna give up vodka.

CARLA: Vodka?

GARY: Yeah. And Jell-O shots.

CARLA: Vodka and Jell-O shots?

GARY: Yep.

CARLA: Vodka and Jell-O shots?

GARY: That's what I'm gonna do.

CARLA: That's all?

GARY: Yeah.

CARLA: Vodka and Jell-O shots?

GARY: Stop saying it like that.

CARLA: That's your whole proposal?

GARY: No, wait—I was gonna give up wine coolers too.

CARLA: You don't drink wine coolers.

GARY: But now I'm not gonna start.

CARLA: Fuck, Gary.

GARY: That's a no?

CARLA: I need you to give up more than vodka and Jell-O shots.

GARY: Don't forget wine coolers.

CARLA: I need more than that.

GARY: I think it's a pretty big thing I'm doing for you.

CARLA: Get out of my face. Leave.

GARY: You want me to leave?

CARLA: Please.

GARY: Fine.

CARLA: Go.

GARY: I know when I'm not wanted.

CARLA: Go now.

GARY: So I'll just leave.

Gary doesn't move. Carla touches him.

CARLA: Tell Michael I'm praying for him, okay?

Gary pulls away, defensive.

GARY: I'm not your message-boy.
CARLA: Is he at the hospital?
GARY: They're doing chemo next week.
CARLA: What if that doesn't work?
GARY: Then they're gonna try a bone marrow transplant. Stop asking so many questions.
CARLA: But do they have a donor? I know it can be hard to find the perfect match.
GARY: They have a donor.
CARLA: Is it David?
GARY: No.
CARLA: Pamela?
GARY: They're incompatible, okay?
CARLA: Then who is it? Gary?
   Who is it?
GARY: Who do you think it is? So shut up already.
CARLA (*realizing*): Oh. Gary—
GARY: You told me to leave.

He goes.

Lights shift.

SCENE TEN

A few weeks later.

Michael's hospital room.

Michael lies in a hospital bed, wearing a knit cap over his now-bald head. David and Pamela sit with him.

DAVID: Your mom and dad are both gonna be here the whole time, so if it hurts, just squeeze my hand, okay?
PAMELA: It's not gonna hurt.
DAVID: He should be prepared—it might hurt a little.
PAMELA: I'm sure he'll be fine.
DAVID (*to Michael*): Squeeze my hand if it hurts, okay?
PAMELA: It's just a blood transfusion.
DAVID: It's a needle.
PAMELA: Don't get him all stressed out—it's nothing.
DAVID: I want him to be prepared.
PAMELA: He's prepared.

(*to Michael*)

You're prepared, right?
MICHAEL: Yeah.

DAVID: Are you nervous?

PAMELA: He's not nervous.

DAVID: You can tell us if you are. We're here for you if you get—

PAMELA: He's not nervous. He said he's not.

DAVID: The problem with children and hospitals is that they often mistake feelings of fear for feelings of pain and feelings of pain for feelings of fear, so pain management becomes difficult. I'm just trying to make sure we have an open dialogue with our son so we can help him when he needs help.

PAMELA: We can have an open dialogue—

DAVID: That's what I'm trying to have.

PAMELA: —without freaking him out.

DAVID: You're the one who's freaking out.

PAMELA: I'm not freaking out.

DAVID: Don't do this in front of Michael.

PAMELA: I'm not doing anything.

MICHAEL: Dad?

DAVID: Yeah?

MICHAEL: I am nervous.

Beat. They register his words.

DAVID: You want me to tell you a story?

MICHAEL: Yeah.

DAVID: Okay. So, once upon a time there was a boy named...

MICHAEL: Michael?

DAVID: Yes, his name was Michael. And at the time of this story, he was only a boy, but he was going to grow up to be a king.

> *Pam puts her right hand under her left arm, feels for something.*

DAVID: But before he could be king, he had to prove to his kingdom that he could be strong like a king.
MICHAEL: Strong like you?
DAVID: Strong like his father, who was king before him.

> *Pam moves her hand from under her arm.*

MICHAEL: How'd he prove he was strong?
DAVID: He had to kill a dragon. But this wasn't just any old dragon.

> *Pam puts her hand back under her arm. She finds something...*

This dragon was the biggest, baddest dragon that ever lived. He breathed fire and he barfed lava.

> *Pam takes her hand away, tries to ignore it. Her breathing intensifies.*

MICHAEL: What did he poop?

DAVID: Hot chunks of cement with nails sticking out of them.

Pam starts to feel her throat.

And when he was flying around, he'd poop in the air and his big dragon droppings would fall on people and smash their heads in. And their dead heads would smell really bad because they'd been killed by poop.

PAMELA (*almost a whimper*): David?

DAVID: Now what do you think the dragon peed?

MICHAEL: Apple juice?

DAVID: Yes!

MICHAEL: Was it good?

PAMELA: David?

DAVID: Surprisingly good. The townspeople sold it at the local market. They were sad that when the dragon died, they wouldn't be able to drink his apple juice anymore—

PAMELA: David?

DAVID: But they figured they'd rather be free from the tyranny of an evil dragon than have good apple juice to drink. And that's when Michael the Prince comes into our story.

PAMELA: David? David? I can't breathe, David, I can't, I can't, my throat, David, my throat, it, it, it, it, oh my, my, oh my god, my throat, my, my, my throat, it's, it's, oh god, god, David, I can't breathe, David, I can't, I can't, I can't—

DAVID: You can breathe.

PAMELA: I can't, I can't, I can't...

DAVID: You can...

PAMELA: Oh my, oh, my, oh my, oh my, oh my, oh my...

DAVID (*falling into caretaker mode*): Don't hyperventilate.

PAMELA: I can't, I can't, I can't, oh god, oh god, oh god, oh god...

DAVID: Breathe. Slow down, breathe.

PAMELA: I can't, I can't, I can't...

DAVID: Breathe.

PAMELA: Breathe, breathe, please, please, breathe, breathe, breathe.

DAVID: That's right.

PAMELA (*slowing down*): Breathe, breathe. Breathe, breathe. Breathe, breathe.

DAVID: That's good.

PAMELA: Breathe.

DAVID: Right.

PAMELA: Breathe.

DAVID: You're doing good.

PAMELA: I am. I'm doing good. Okay, I'm sorry. Okay. Okay.

DAVID: You're better now?

PAMELA: Oh, god, I can't believe I just did that.

DAVID: Pamela, look at me. Are you better now?

PAMELA: Yes. I'm better now.

DAVID: Then I want you to go home.

PAMELA: What? Why?

DAVID: It'll be better for Michael if you're not here right now.

PAMELA: I'm his mother.

DAVID: Go home, Pamela.

PAMELA: Michael needs me. You need me, don't you, Michael?

Beat.

You want me here.

Michael doesn't respond.

Michael, you want me here. Right? Tell me you want me here.

MICHAEL: Mom...

PAMELA: Say it, Michael.

DAVID: Pamela, stop.

PAMELA (*to David*): I'm not doing anything wrong.

MICHAEL: But Mom...

PAMELA: Hold on, Michael. Your father thinks I'm doing something wrong. But I'm not. I'm not. He needs me.

MICHAEL: Mom...You should listen to Dad.

PAMELA: What?

MICHAEL: It's okay if you go home.

PAMELA: You want me to go?

MICHAEL: I love you, but...I think it'd be better if you weren't here.

PAMELA: Okay.

She walks to the door.

Okay. Okay. Okay.

She stands in the doorway.

David and Michael just look at her.
Pamela doesn't move.

After several beats...

MICHAEL: Mom? You're making me nervous. I need you to leave. Please.

Pamela runs out.

Lights shift.

SCENE ELEVEN

A few days later.

The hospital cafeteria.

Pamela and Dr. Brown sit at a table, eating Jell-O.

PAMELA: Thank you for meeting me down here.
BROWN: I was hungry.
PAMELA: Me too.

    They each take a bite of Jell-O.

BROWN: How is he?
PAMELA: Hm?
BROWN: Michael.
PAMELA: What?
BROWN: Your son.
PAMELA: I know.
BROWN: How's he doing?
PAMELA: He's, um...you know.

    Pamela finishes her Jell-O cup, opens another.

You want another Jell-O?

BROWN: I'm still working on this one.

PAMELA: Okey-dokey.

BROWN: I spoke with Dr. Carlson.

PAMELA: You did?

BROWN: Yeah. He said Michael was responding well to the chemo.

PAMELA: Hey, it looks like you're done with that Jell-O to me.

BROWN: Pamela.

PAMELA: Just say "when"—

BROWN: Pam—

PAMELA: —'cause I've got another cup with your name on it.

BROWN: Are you listening to me?

PAMELA: Yes.

BROWN: I just...hope...you're keeping his spirits up.

PAMELA: Please, could you...

BROWN: It's so important.

PAMELA: I don't wanna talk about him right now, okay? Oh my god, I am so hungry.

She starts to eat another Jell-O.

BROWN: Okay, so, uh...If you don't want to talk about Michael, what are we doing here?

PAMELA: I don't know.

BROWN: I'm here if you need me.

PAMELA: Thanks. I guess that's, yeah—that's why I called you.

BROWN: Because you needed me.

PAMELA: Yes...uh, Dr. Brown? Are you...are you married?

BROWN: Kind of.

PAMELA: What's that mean?

BROWN: Call me Tim.

PAMELA: Okay, so, Tim, um...

BROWN: Yeah?

PAMELA: What do you mean when you say you're "kind of" married?

BROWN: I'm not married.

PAMELA: You're not?

BROWN: No.

PAMELA: What about your ring?

BROWN: Okay, I am.

PAMELA: Which is it?

BROWN: I have a wife.

PAMELA: But you don't want to have a wife?

BROWN: Well, I love her...but...

PAMELA: But what?

BROWN: You know...

PAMELA: No, I don't.

BROWN: But...I'm open to what you're suggesting.

PAMELA: You are?

BROWN: Yeah.

PAMELA: How do you even know...

BROWN: Come on...

PAMELA: ...what I'm suggesting?

BROWN: I'm not stupid.

PAMELA: I didn't say you were stupid.

BROWN: A woman calls up her son's pediatrician...

PAMELA: So?

BROWN: ...she doesn't want to talk about her son...

PAMELA: I can't.

BROWN: ...who's sick...

PAMELA: I just can't.

BROWN: ...who's really, really sick...

PAMELA: Don't say that.

BROWN: ...she wants to talk about "something else"...

PAMELA: I do.

BROWN: Well, there's only one other thing to talk about.

PAMELA: Okay.

BROWN: Am I right—

PAMELA: Yeah.

BROWN: —or am I right? I wanna hear you say it.

PAMELA: Say what?

BROWN: What you want to do.

PAMELA: I'm not sure I still—

BROWN: Say it.

PAMELA: Don't be so—

BROWN: Come on.

PAMELA: —aggressive.

BROWN: Say. It.

PAMELA: This was a bad idea.

BROWN: You're not gonna chicken out, are you?

PAMELA: No, I—

BROWN: Come on, Pam.

PAMELA: Wait—

BROWN: Tell me what you wanna do.

PAMELA: But I don't anymore.

BROWN: Yeah, you do. Come on.

PAMELA: You're my son's doctor.

BROWN: Not anymore. Dr. Carlson's his doctor.

PAMELA: I know, but—

BROWN: You called me.

PAMELA: Right.

BROWN: For a reason.

PAMELA: But Dr. Brown—

BROWN: Tim.

PAMELA: Dr. Brown—

BROWN: Call me Tim.

PAMELA: But Tim—

BROWN: No buts.

PAMELA: No, you don't understand.

BROWN: I do.

PAMELA: I changed my mind.

BROWN: You called me—

PAMELA: Yes.

BROWN: So stop—

PAMELA: No.

BROWN: —beating around the bush—

PAMELA: I'm not.

BROWN: —and tell me—

PAMELA: Please.

BROWN: —what you wanna do to me.

PAMELA: I wanna fuck you. Alright? I wanna fuck you. There. I said it. Okay? So could you just shut up for one second? I know you're married. But you knew what I was going to say and you made me say it, so I have to assume you've done this before. You have, haven't you? Well I haven't done this. I don't do this. This isn't my thing. Because I'm married too, to the greatest guy in the world. I mean, he's the best. Like, he might actually be the greatest guy in the world. I'm barely exaggerating. And me? I mean, me? I'm not the greatest. I'm not. Like, right now, while I'm here with you, my husband is upstairs with our sick son. Because that's how good he is. And I'm here with you, because that's how bad I am. He's upstairs with Michael. And I wanna fuck you. And I got the distinct impression that you wanted to fuck me, too, when we sat down together, but, you know, the more we talk, the more I talk, the more I feel like maybe I read this situation wrong and you don't want to fuck me and I'm making a fool of myself. Am I making a fool of myself? Do you not want to fuck me? Is that what's happening right now? Say something. Don't leave me hanging here. Just don't. Leave me. Hanging. Okay? Please? Tim? Dr. Tim? Tim Brown? Dr. Tim Brown? That's a boring name. You know, when I called you, when I asked you to meet me here, I didn't know what was gonna happen. I didn't think I was gonna say anything. But then you made me say it. And now I can't take it back. So, now, like: what the hell, you know? Life's too short. So do you wanna fuck me or not?

BROWN: *When.*

PAMELA: Really? You do? That's a yes?

BROWN: No, I want more Jell-O.

PAMELA: What?

BROWN: You told me to say "when" when I wanted more Jell-O.

PAMELA: Oh.

> *She hands him a cup of Jell-O. He eats it. Pamela stares at him for a beat.*

PAMELA: Your foot is in my crotch.

BROWN: Yeah.

PAMELA: Your sock. That's your sock. You took off your shoe.

BROWN: Well, yeah—I didn't want to put my shoe in your pussy.

PAMELA: So that's...that's...that's a, a, a—

BROWN: That's a yes.

> *Lights shift.*

SCENE TWELVE

A church basement.

Jeannie stands at a refreshment table, fixing herself a cup of coffee.

Gary enters, looks around.

JEANNIE: You look lost.
    Yoo-hoo? Hello?

Gary looks at Jeannie.

    Yes, I'm talking to you.
GARY: Is this a church?
JEANNIE: Yes.
GARY: I thought this was supposed to be AA.
JEANNIE: You're a little late—
GARY: Shit, I missed it?
JEANNIE: Yeah.
GARY: But there's people in that room...
JEANNIE: That's OA.
GARY: OA?
JEANNIE: Overeaters Anonymous.
GARY: Fat people?

JEANNIE: Not all of us. I should be in there, but I needed some coffee. It's my last poison.

GARY: So there's really no more AA meetings here today?

JEANNIE: Sorry. It's a bummer you missed it, we had a really good meeting today.

GARY: So you go to AA too?

JEANNIE: Oh, yeah.

GARY: You must be really fucked up.

JEANNIE: Pretty fucked up, yeah.

GARY: When's the last time you had a drink?

JEANNIE: Just over twelve years ago.

GARY: Holy shit—and you still go to meetings?

JEANNIE (*shrugging, with a smile*): I want a drink right now so bad it's killing me.

GARY: I'm fucked up too. At least my wife thinks so.

JEANNIE: What do you think?

GARY: I think I need to inject some fucking change into my life, but I don't know how. I didn't realize this was in a church.

JEANNIE: You don't like churches?

GARY: They give me the creeps.

JEANNIE: The Wilshire meeting's not in a church. If you leave right now, I bet you could still catch it.

GARY: Nah, it's okay. Gas is too expensive.

Jeannie grabs a glazed donut.

JEANNIE: Hey, you wanna split a donut with me?

GARY: Sure.

JEANNIE: They're from the NA meeting. There aren't usually any leftovers, and when there are, they usually throw them away before the OA's get here, but today's our lucky day. Krispy Kreme's better than sex, most of the time.

She gives Gary his half.

I really shouldn't eat the whole thing, though.

She motions at the OA meeting.

And don't tell anyone in there that I ate this.

They eat their donut.

So, are you clean at all? Or do you just wanna be?

GARY: Oh, I'm clean. Shit is hard.

JEANNIE: How long?

GARY: A coupl'a weeks.

JEANNIE: What made you—

GARY: I had to. My nephew. He's all fucked up medically. It's a long story, but it's 'cause of that I had to get straight.

JEANNIE: I'm sorry about your nephew.

GARY: And my wife's into God now, which is its own ball of wax.

JEANNIE: She left you?

GARY: How'd you know?

JEANNIE: I could just tell. You have that look, like someone shot you. My husband left me once—

GARY: Sorry.

JEANNIE: Nothing to be sorry about. We got back together a year later. It's a long story, but now he's my rock, and I try to be his.

GARY: So you think I have a shot with Carla?

JEANNIE: You always gotta have hope, right?

GARY: I guess.

JEANNIE: Do you pray?

GARY: Oh, you're not one of them, are you?

JEANNIE: What's wrong with being "one of them"?

GARY: I don't believe in God.

JEANNIE: Check out Corinthians 6:19 through 6:20.

GARY: Corinthawhat?

JEANNIE: It's from the Bible. I find it helpful. When I'm struggling.

GARY: So you *are* one of them.

JEANNIE: I don't know what I am. Look, I gotta go. I'm late for work.

GARY: Night shift?

JEANNIE: Yeah, I work at the hospital. Nothing special. But listen, before I go, can I just...

She collects her thoughts.

...I don't know if I believe in "God" either, the way people define him. Like he's a "man," or a "being," or whatever. But I've been through some dark stuff, and when I was really at the bottom of it...after my husband left me, when he took the kids...I didn't know what to do, so...I prayed. I figured it couldn't hurt, right? At least not like all the other things. And it's hard to describe how, but it helped. I'm not telling you to believe in a man with a big white beard in the clouds. That's not who I talk to. It's more like: there's something inside all of us, something bigger than us. And when you pray, you tap into that bigger thing. This collective energy that we all put out there: that's God to me. That's who I talk to. And when I do, I feel...a little less alone. At least that's what it does for me.

She gives Gary a shy smile.

Anyway, thanks for sharing the donut with me.
GARY: I won't tell anyone you ate some.
JEANNIE: Good. Thanks.

Jeannie exits.

Lights shift.

SCENE THIRTEEN

Pam's living room, empty. Carla enters.

CARLA: Hello? Anyone here?

Pamela enters.

PAMELA: Carla, thank you so much for coming.
CARLA: No problem.
PAMELA: David's car's in the shop. I didn't know what to do. I just have to pick him up from work and then I'll be back.
CARLA: It's okay.
PAMELA: I won't be long.
CARLA: Don't get a speeding ticket.
PAMELA: Michael's asleep. I could've left him, but it'd be bad if he woke up and no one was here.
CARLA: I'm happy to help.
PAMELA: How long has it been? A couple of months?
CARLA: Since I kicked Gary out. So, yeah.
PAMELA: How are you? How've you been?
CARLA: I'm fine, I'm...I can't believe you're the one asking me how I'm doing.
PAMELA: Well, I haven't seen you.
CARLA: How are you, Pam?
PAMELA: I'm...I don't know...I wish it would stop raining.

CARLA: I meant, how are you coping with Michael...?

PAMELA: Right, of course. Yeah, not good. Before I go, do you want some coffee or something?

CARLA: I'm off caffeine.

PAMELA: I have decaf.

CARLA: I can't drink decaf. The taste of it makes me want caffeine, which makes me want cocaine. When I got clean, I had to cut everything off at the source.

PAMELA: Yeah, I should give up caffeine too.

CARLA: 'Cause you're addicted?

PAMELA: No, 'cause it causes cancer.

CARLA: You're joking.

PAMELA: Why would I joke about something like that?

CARLA: I don't know.

Awkward beat.

Is there anything I should know? In case Michael wakes up.

PAMELA: Speaking of cancer...

Now I'm joking.

CARLA: It wasn't funny.

PAMELA: He's asleep. He probably won't wake up.

CARLA: But if he does?

PAMELA: He can watch TV. Or play video games. Whatever he wants.

CARLA: But is there any medication he needs?

PAMELA: It's in the kitchen.

CARLA: Don't you think I should know that?

PAMELA: Michael knows where it is.

CARLA: I just want to be helpful. If he needs me...Is Gary here?

PAMELA: No.

CARLA: How is he?

PAMELA: He's good.

CARLA: Yeah?

PAMELA: He's getting clean.

CARLA: You mean he's off vodka and Jell-O shots?

PAMELA: He's trying to get off everything. I think.

CARLA: What's the punch line?

PAMELA: He's gonna donate his bone marrow to Michael.

CARLA: Wait, he's really doing that? I thought that was just something Gary made up.

PAMELA: They're doing it sometime next week.

CARLA: I don't know what to say. That's...

PAMELA: David's waiting. I have to go. I'm waiting for a call from Michael's doctor. So answer the phone if it rings.

CARLA: What's his name?

PAMELA: Dr. Carlson. If he calls, tell him I'll be right back.

CARLA: Sure.

Pamela exits.

The phone rings.

CARLA: Pam!

But Pamela's already gone. Carla answers the phone.

Hello?

In another part of the stage, we see Dr. Brown on the other line.

BROWN: Hey there.
CARLA: Hi, may I ask who's calling?
BROWN: This is your doctor speaking.
CARLA: Dr. Carlson?
BROWN: You want me to pretend I'm Dr. Carlson?
CARLA (*confused*): Sure...?
BROWN: You think Dr. Carlson's hot, don't you?
CARLA: Excuse me? Could you...
BROWN: What?
CARLA: I don't know who you are.
BROWN: You want me to be a stranger? Is that the game you wanna play today?
CARLA: I think you have the wrong number.
BROWN: Pamela?

Carla looks at the phone, shocked.

Pamela?

She puts the phone back to her ear...

CARLA: Yes?
BROWN: Can you not talk right now?

...and decides...

CARLA: I can talk...
BROWN: Is your husband there?

...to play along.

CARLA: My husband's not here.
BROWN: Then take off your panties.

She doesn't move.

CARLA: Okay. They're off.
BROWN: Put your finger in your pussy, then take it out and lick it.

Oh my god.

CARLA: Okay...
BROWN: That tastes good, huh?

CARLA: Really good.

BROWN: Now pretend you're sitting on my face.

I wanna eat you up.

You sitting on me?

CARLA: I'm sitting.

BROWN: Your pussy tastes so fucking good. Don't you love it when I eat your pussy?

CARLA: Look, I can't do this.

BROWN: Let me hear how much you love it when I eat your pussy.

CARLA: I'm not—

BROWN: I want you to tell me how much you love it.

CARLA: You don't understand—

BROWN: Tell me.

CARLA: I'm not Pamela.

BROWN: I don't care who you are.

CARLA: I understand that, but—

BROWN: I wanna hear you moan.

CARLA: I'm her sister-in-law. I played along because—

BROWN: You wanted to play with my cock.

CARLA: Shut up for one second. Shut the fuck up and listen to me.

BROWN: I like it when you take charge.

CARLA: Shut up and listen! I'm married to Pamela's brother. Her husband is my friend. I played along because I wanted to see where you were going with all of your...pussy talk. But you're disgusting and you're going to hell—

BROWN: Yeah, tell me I'm dirty.

CARLA: I'm done with this conversation.

She hangs up the phone.

Michael! Get down here!

Lights shift.

SCENE FOURTEEN

Later that night.

David stands outside Carla's apartment. The door opens.

CARLA: Hi, David.

DAVID: Michael's inside? He's fine? He's—

CARLA: He's asleep.

DAVID: I read your note.

CARLA: Pam read it too?

DAVID: Yeah. Oh, yeah. I left her, I think.

CARLA: Oh my god, you did?

DAVID: Tell me what happened, exactly. Can you do that?

CARLA: After Pam left to pick you up, the phone rang. I picked it up. It was Michael's doctor.

DAVID: Which one?

CARLA: I thought it was Dr. Carlson, but he asked if I wanted to pretend he was Dr. Carlson, so I don't know.

DAVID: Then what?

CARLA: He thought I was Pam. And then he started saying these nasty things. Things he wanted to do to me...to her. Things he'd already done to her. He kept talking about her...her pussy. He described eating...her pussy...in detail. It was disgusting. That's all. I'm sorry, David. It's awful.

DAVID: That's everything that happened?

CARLA: Then I wrote the note and I brought Michael here. I'm sorry, David. It's so awful that she would do something like this.

DAVID: No, it's...it's good.

CARLA: What do you mean?

DAVID: Well, it sucks that Pam's fuckin' around. That sucks. But... I'm glad I know.

CARLA: You don't feel bad?

DAVID: No. I don't.

Beat.

I don't.

CARLA: But what did Pamela say after you read the note? Did she explain herself? Did she—

DAVID: Let's stop talking about her. She's the only person I've talked about for ten years and I don't want to talk about her anymore. It's my turn to be selfish.

CARLA: Okay. So...how do you feel?

DAVID: I feel horny.

CARLA: David...

DAVID: You asked how I felt.

CARLA: I meant emotionally.

DAVID: I need to get laid. That's, like, three emotions.

CARLA: I won't have sex with you—

DAVID: Not even a little?

> *David moves closer, touches her hand.*

CARLA: You're touching my hand.

> *David leans in and kisses her.*

> *She pulls away.*

David...stop.

> *David stops.*

Well this is awkward.

> *David kisses her again. Carla pushes him off.*

Jesus, David!
DAVID: What?
CARLA: I said stop, okay? Pour some water on yourself. Jesus.
DAVID: Sorry.
CARLA: Look, why don't I go get Michael? And then you can go.
DAVID: You're gonna come around, Carla. You're gonna realize you want me.
CARLA: I don't know about that.
DAVID: But maybe?

CARLA: I'm gonna pray for you—that's what I'm gonna do. And I'm gonna pray for Pamela.

DAVID: Don't waste it on us—just pray for Michael.

CARLA: I already am.

DAVID: Thanks...and you have my number. If you come around. Oh, and can he sleep here tonight? I don't want to wake him. I'll pick him up in the morning?

CARLA: That's fine, yeah. But David—don't give up on Pamela. You never know—maybe she'll change.

DAVID: She already did change.

Lights shift.

SCENE FIFTEEN

Several days later.

Gary's kitchen.

Pamela and Gary sit at the table. Gary reads the Bible. Pamela stares at him.

GARY: Stop staring at me.

PAMELA: I'm thirsty.

GARY: There's water in the tap.

PAMELA: I want some tea.

GARY: Go to the store.

PAMELA: You don't have tea?

GARY: I told you, there's water—

PAMELA: —in the tap. I know. I don't want tap. I want tea.

GARY: It's good to have dreams.

PAMELA: Why are you reading the Bible?

GARY: I don't have to believe it—I just have to show Carla that I'm trying to believe it.

PAMELA: Do you have any lemons? I could heat up some lemon water.

GARY: I don't have lemons.

PAMELA: Then what do you have?

GARY: I told you. I have tap water.

PAMELA: That's all?

GARY: I just moved into this place. Give me a break.

PAMELA: Do you have Tylenol, at least?

GARY: Listen, I'll let you stay here. I'll let you live here for as long as you want. Until David invites you back home. Or until you get your own place. I won't ever pressure you to leave. You can think of this place as your own home, I swear.

PAMELA: Thanks, Gary.

GARY: But I haven't done any shopping yet, so shut the fuck up, okay? How's Michael doing?

PAMELA: What do you mean?

GARY: I mean, is the chemo working like gangbusters? Is he ready for my bone marrow?

PAMELA: I don't know. Call David.

GARY: You need to call him, Pam.

PAMELA: He doesn't wanna talk to me. What do you want to do tonight?

GARY: I don't know.

PAMELA: You wanna watch TV?

GARY: I don't have a TV.

PAMELA: Where'd you get a Bible?

GARY: I stole it from the Ali Baba Motel down the street. You could read it if you wanted to. We could take turns.

PAMELA: No, thanks.

GARY: It's weird language. I keep reading the same page. "Or know ye not that your body is a temple of the Holy Spirit which is in you, which ye have from God?" And blah blah blah. You think you can make some sense out of that?

PAMELA: I don't need to win back Carla, so I'm fine, thanks.

GARY: It's from Corinthians.

PAMELA: I don't know what that means.

GARY: And what's all the "ye" shit? That's what I want to know.

PAMELA: God, my life sucks.

GARY: You won't be living with me forever.

PAMELA: You think David'll take me back? What if I die first?

GARY: Pam, you're the healthiest person I've ever met.

PAMELA: I'm not, though.

GARY: You've never really had anything wrong with you.

PAMELA: Everything's wrong with me. I'm prone to cancer.

GARY: That's stupid, you're not.

PAMELA: What if there's something in the house? Something like radiation? That gave the cancer to Michael? I was in that house more than he ever was. I probably got the cancer too.

GARY: Stop saying that.

PAMELA: But what if? I don't want to die, Gary.

GARY: Wow. I've heard you say all of these things before, but this is amazing.

PAMELA: What is?

GARY: I just realized.

PAMELA: Realized what?

GARY: I don't like you when I'm sober. You're awful.

PAMELA: How can you say that?

GARY: You're mean. All you care about is yourself.

PAMELA: That's not true.

GARY: Yeah, it is.

PAMELA: It's not.

GARY: Is too.

PAMELA: No...is not.

GARY: It is, Pam.

PAMELA: Look, I'm gonna go to the grocery store. My throat hurts. I need to get some tea. But I'll get you some stuff too. What do you need from the market? I'll get it for you. See? You're my brother, I care about you. What do you need?

He doesn't respond, so she grabs her purse and exits.

Lights shift.

SCENE SIXTEEN

An hour later.

A sterile white hospital room.

Pamela enters, holding groceries. She's followed in by Dr. Brown.

PAMELA: I wasn't sure if you'd still be here this late.
BROWN (*undoing his tie*): Paperwork.
PAMELA: I was out shopping for my brother.

She puts the groceries down.

I was just down the street. So I thought I'd stop by. I had to see you.
BROWN: Thank god you did.

He kisses her, lifts her up onto the examination table.

PAMELA: Do you...um, do you...

He lifts up her skirt, kissing her thighs.

Do you like me?

BROWN: Yeah, you're fucking hot.

PAMELA: I know you like fucking me, but...

He unbuttons his pants.

Do you like me as a person?

BROWN: Fuck, yeah.

PAMELA: Wait. Feel my neck.

BROWN: Oh, yeah, baby.

PAMELA: Put your hands on my neck.

BROWN: What do you want me to do with them?

PAMELA: Just feel my neck.

BROWN: You're into asphyxiation?

PAMELA: No, I just want you to put your hands on my neck and feel it.

BROWN: Feel for what?

PAMELA: My lymph nodes. Feel them. Are they swollen? You didn't feel my neck. Put your hands—what's wrong?

BROWN: No, that's too—

PAMELA: Just tell me—are they swollen?

BROWN: That's too fucked up.

PAMELA: I just need to know.

BROWN: Is that how you get off?

PAMELA: No, they feel swollen, I just—

BROWN: They're not swollen.

PAMELA: You didn't even feel them.

Dr. Brown buckles up his pants.

He examines the lymph nodes in her neck.

Well?
BROWN: They're not swollen.
PAMELA: But my throat hurts.

Beat.

Don't look at me like that.
That's how David looks at me.
Don't—
Just—come on, let's fuck.
BROWN: I don't want to anymore.
PAMELA: Forget I said anything. Just fuck me.
BROWN: I don't think I could get it up for you anymore.
PAMELA: Please?
BROWN: This is wrong. This is...

Beat.

I see sick kids every day. Most of them aren't too bad: it's just the flu, or a cold, or maybe they have the chicken pox. Nothing too serious. Some of them though, some of them have real illnesses. Like your son. Bad things are gonna happen to them. But these kids...these sick kids...they're troopers. They really are, most of them. Maybe it's because they're so young they don't know to be afraid. But whatever it is, they have faith. They have hope. They have guts. And then there are people like you. Healthy people like you make me sick. You waste my time. You think there's something wrong with your body, but it's all in your head. Why don't you just...just...leave being sick to the sick people. You know? Just leave it to the sick people.

Lights shift.

SCENE SEVENTEEN

Several days later.

A hospital room.

Gary lies in bed, in a hospital gown. Michael sits in a wheelchair.

MICHAEL: You ready for this?

GARY: Yeah. How 'bout you? You ready? You know what's gonna happen?

MICHAEL: They're gonna harvest your bone marrow, then give it to me.

GARY: Exactly.

MICHAEL: How are they gonna give it to me?

GARY: I don't know—probably a needle.

MICHAEL: I can't believe I'm gonna have your bone marrow. It's so weird.

GARY: You better hope I don't have cooties.

MICHAEL: Cooties aren't real.

GARY: Okay, good, 'cause I thought I had 'em.

Carla appears in the doorway.

MICHAEL: So, Uncle Gary...about your bone marrow.

GARY: What about it?

MICHAEL: Are you sure I should take it?

GARY: Yeah, I want you to have it.

MICHAEL: But are you gonna die?

GARY: Not today.

MICHAEL: Am I gonna die?

GARY: You might.

MICHAEL: Really?

    Tomorrow?

GARY: It could happen.

MICHAEL: That would suck.

GARY: It would really suck.

MICHAEL: Hey, Uncle Gary? I don't want to die.

GARY: I know, kid. But here's the thing: without my bone marrow, you're definitely gonna die. But with it, you're back to maybe. So, I'll give it to you and we'll cross our fingers. And I've been praying, so maybe that'll help. You never know.

CARLA (*from the doorway*): Hey...Michael...

MICHAEL: Aunt Carla!

CARLA: Hi, sweetie. How are you feeling?

MICHAEL: I'm okay.

GARY: I was starting to think I was never gonna see you again.

> *Carla doesn't look at Gary. She can't, not yet. She stays with Michael.*

CARLA: I heard today was the big day. Are you ready?

GARY: You aren't talking to me?

MICHAEL: It isn't my big day, it's Gary's big day. They don't give me his bone marrow until tomorrow.

CARLA: They don't do it right away?

MICHAEL: No.

CARLA: Oh, I didn't realize...

GARY: You hate me still? That's why you won't look at me? Carla?

CARLA: I don't hate you. I never hated you.

GARY: Then why won't you look at me?

She finally looks at him.

CARLA: Hi Gary.

GARY: Hey. So, listen, you know: I'm trying to change, okay? Like, I don't know if I actually *have*, but I'm trying really hard.

MICHAEL: He's been reading the Bible.

GARY: Trying to. I don't really get it. Most of the time I'm reading, I'm like: what the fuck? But every once in a while I have these moments where I'm reading and I can't help but be like, "wow." You know what I'm talking about? You get that?

CARLA: Yeah. I get those moments too.

GARY: And I was thinking...those other things you wanted me to do, to give up...I kind of did those things, mostly. So now...

CARLA: It's hard.

GARY: Yeah, it's really tough, and what I'm trying to say is, I went to AA, I went to this meeting, the one on Wilshire...

CARLA: You did?

GARY: Yeah.

CARLA: You did that for me?

GARY: Of course, and the thing is, I really fucking hated it, the meeting, I hated it so bad, so—

CARLA: It's okay, Gary, you don't have to—

GARY: No, let me finish. So I was thinking. You're here, and I'm here, and we're both at this place that's hard for us—

CARLA: Really fucking hard—

GARY: Right, it's really fucking hard, and I was thinking, maybe, we could be, like, each other's support group, you know? It's not the worst idea in the world, is it?

> *Carla's getting emotional. She shakes her head, no.*

GARY: So you'll do it with me? Even though I didn't change as much as you wanted me to?

CARLA: Shut up, Gary.

GARY: Why do you gotta be like that? Why do you gotta—

CARLA: Because...there is nothing defective about your character.

> *She kisses him and he finally gets it: she likes me again.*

CARLA: Now. So—I hear you've got some bone marrow to donate.

GARY: Yeah. And it's gonna kick some fuckin' ass.

Lights shift.

SCENE EIGHTEEN

Later that night.

The hospital gift shop.

Jeannie, the sales clerk, sits at the counter. David stands at a kiosk, reading "Get Well" cards. Pamela enters.

PAMELA: David...

DAVID: Pam.

PAMELA: What are you...

DAVID: Michael's taking a nap.

PAMELA: I was gonna buy some candy and then go upstairs. Where's Gary? Have they already—

DAVID: They just did it. He's fine.

PAMELA: And the transplant?

DAVID: It's tomorrow morning.

PAMELA: So I didn't miss it...I didn't expect to see you in here.

DAVID: I wanted something to read.

PAMELA: "Get Well" cards?

DAVID: They make me feel good.

PAMELA: I was gonna go up and see him, if that's okay.

DAVID: It's okay.

PAMELA: Will he want to see me?

DAVID: I think so.

PAMELA: I wanted to get something here first. Bring him something.

DAVID: Do you mind if I go home then? For a couple of hours? I could use a shower.

PAMELA: Sure.

DAVID: I'm just kind of beefy.

PAMELA: I'll stay with Michael.

DAVID: Okay, thanks.

PAMELA: Hey, before you go—

DAVID: Yeah?

She grabs a greeting card.

PAMELA: "I can't bear to be without you."

DAVID: What?

PAMELA: I picked it at random. I just wanted to help you feel good. There's a picture of a bear on the card, that's why it says I can't bear to be without you.

DAVID: Clever.

PAMELA: How mad at me are you? On a scale of one to ten?

DAVID: I told you, I'm not mad at you.

PAMELA: But you left me.

DAVID: You fucked around.

PAMELA: You should be mad. I mean, don't you kind of hate me? Just a little bit? Because it's okay, I fucked up, I deserve it.

DAVID: I'm not mad at you. I'm more...sad at you...God, that sounded really stupid.

PAMELA: No, it was cute.

DAVID: It was embarrassing.

PAMELA: You should write it down...

DAVID: ...and send it to Hallmark?

PAMELA: Yeah.

> *Beat.*

I am sorry, David. You've always been there for me. Even though I haven't always been sick—and I know I haven't been—you've always been there. Oh, god, what I've put you and Michael through...I'm a bad person, aren't I?

DAVID: Don't say that. Why do you always say things like that?

PAMELA: Aren't I, though? Just...you know me better than anyone. So tell me—am I a bad person?

DAVID: No, you're not a bad person. You're just a bad mom.

> *David exits. Pamela looks at Jeannie.*

> *She forces a smile for the stranger.*

PAMELA: Sorry you had to hear all of that.

JEANNIE: It's okay.

PAMELA: I'm Pamela.

JEANNIE: Hi, Pamela. I'm Jeannie. Tough night?

PAMELA: No, I'm good.

JEANNIE: Really?

PAMELA: No.

JEANNIE: You just say you're good? To trick yourself?

PAMELA: Yeah, I thought I'd give that a try.

JEANNIE: Fake it 'til you make it?

PAMELA: Yeah.

JEANNIE: Well, let me know if I can help you find anything.

PAMELA: Are you a mom?

JEANNIE: Yeah.

PAMELA: How many kids do you have?

JEANNIE: Two.

PAMELA: Boys? Girls?

JEANNIE: One of each. Katie's eighteen and Tyler's ten.

PAMELA: My son's ten, too.

JEANNIE: His name's Michael, right?

Pamela nods.

Sorry—I couldn't help but overhear.

PAMELA: It's okay.

JEANNIE: Do you mind if I ask how old you are? You don't look old enough to have a ten-year-old.

PAMELA: I'm not old enough. I'm twenty-eight.

JEANNIE: So you were—

PAMELA: Eighteen, yeah.

JEANNIE: No, that's not old enough.

PAMELA: Tell Katie to use a condom.

JEANNIE: We've had the talk.

PAMELA: Have it again.

JEANNIE: Okay.

    So, your son, he...

PAMELA: He's upstairs.

JEANNIE: Do you mind if I ask...

PAMELA: I don't mind.

JEANNIE: What does he have?

PAMELA: He has leukemia.

JEANNIE: Oh. Oh, god.

PAMELA: Yeah, he has leukemia.

JEANNIE: I'm so sorry.

PAMELA: I've never actually said that out loud before.

JEANNIE: How bad is it?

PAMELA: It's...it's...um. It's...it's pretty bad.

JEANNIE: Oh, honey...

Jeannie gives Pamela a hug.

    It's okay, let it out.

PAMELA: I'm sorry.

JEANNIE: You gotta cry when you gotta cry.

PAMELA: I guess.

JEANNIE: That man who was in here before...

PAMELA: My husband. David.

JEANNIE: What he said, when he left...I'm sure he didn't mean it.

PAMELA: No, he did.

JEANNIE: You seem like a good mom to me.

PAMELA: No, he was right.

JEANNIE: You're too hard on yourself.

PAMELA: No, David's a good dad. He should know. But me? Me...

She shakes her head.

...Listen, I don't want to talk about myself anymore. I should go upstairs in case Michael wakes up. But I want to get something for him first. Something that might cheer him up. That'll make him smile. Can you help me find something?

JEANNIE: What does he like?

PAMELA: I, uh...I don't have a fucking clue.

Lights shift.

SCENE NINETEEN

The next morning.

Michael's hospital room.

Michael's asleep. Pamela sits at his side. Michael opens his eyes.

MICHAEL: Hi, mom.

PAMELA: Hey.

MICHAEL: What are you doing here?

PAMELA: Seeing you.

MICHAEL: Where's dad?

PAMELA: He went to get something to eat.

MICHAEL: Oh, okay.

PAMELA: I told him you'd be fine...Are you fine?

MICHAEL: Yeah.

PAMELA: Good. He'll be back in a little bit. Before your procedure.
    Oh, and I saw Gary. They got his bone marrow.

MICHAEL: How is he?

PAMELA: He's down in the cafeteria. He's eating. He's doing good.
    Really good.

Beat.

MICHAEL: How long have you been here?

PAMELA: Since last night.

MICHAEL: I was asleep the whole time?

PAMELA: Yeah.

MICHAEL: I'm sorry.

PAMELA: No, it's okay.

Beat.

They put you in a new room. You got a better view.

Michael nods.

Have they been letting you watch TV?

MICHAEL: Yeah.

PAMELA: See anything good?

Michael shakes his head no.

PAMELA: Hey, guess what?

MICHAEL: What?

PAMELA: I got a new job.

MICHAEL: Really?

PAMELA: Yeah, at this new Italian restaurant. It's fancy, so I'm gonna make a lot of money in tips.

MICHAEL: Cool.

PAMELA: It's like I'm starting over. It's a whole new job. I'm gonna start over from scratch.

MICHAEL: That's what you wanted.

PAMELA: Well, not really. What I really wanted was something completely different, not another restaurant job. I mean, who's to say at this new restaurant I'm not gonna get stuck in the same rut I was stuck in before? Who's to say this new restaurant isn't gonna suck even more? You never know. When I said I wanted a new job, I didn't mean at another restaurant. I meant I wanted something totally different, totally—no. Sorry, no. We don't need to talk about that.

So, um...

She doesn't know what to say.

Hey, want something sweet? I got you some candy downstairs.

Okay, I didn't know what your favorite candy bar was, so—

MICHAEL: It's Milky Way.

PAMELA: Really?

MICHAEL: Yeah.

PAMELA: Okay, well, I wasn't sure, so I got one of everything.

MICHAEL: Thanks.

PAMELA: Can I ask you a question?

MICHAEL: You're my mom.

PAMELA: So?

MICHAEL: So you can ask me anything. That's what moms do.

PAMELA: I never thought about it that way. Okay, so: here goes.

> *Pamela climbs up into the bed, puts her arm around him.*

    Why do you like baseball?

MICHAEL: I don't know.

PAMELA: Sure you do. What's your favorite thing about it?

MICHAEL: I like running.

PAMELA: Why?

MICHAEL: Because I'm fast. It feels really good to run really fast.

PAMELA: Are you faster than Superman?

MICHAEL: He's faster than a speeding bullet, so no. But I try.

PAMELA: I never knew you liked running so much. Okay, another question. What do you want to be when you grow up? And you can't say "faster than Superman."

MICHAEL: I want to be a paleontologist.

PAMELA: I knew that!

MICHAEL: Dinosaurs are cool.

PAMELA: I bet there's one that hasn't been discovered yet.

MICHAEL: I bet.

PAMELA: Maybe you could discover it.

MICHAEL: That'd be so cool.

PAMELA: Wouldn't it?

MICHAEL: Yeah.

PAMELA: They could call it a Michael-a-sauras.

MICHEAL: It'd probably be an herbivore.

PAMELA: Why do you say that?

MICHAEL: Because if it hasn't been discovered yet, then its bones are probably deeper in the soil, which means it's really old. And if it's that old, then it was extinct before a lot of other, stronger dinosaurs. And it probably became extinct because it was eaten by them. It was eaten by the stronger carnivores.

PAMELA: Wow.

MICHAEL: Survival of the fittest.

PAMELA: How'd you get so smart?

Michael shrugs.

You like school, don't you?

MICHAEL: Yeah. I'm a dork.

PAMELA: Don't say that!

MICHAEL: It's okay, I don't mind being a dork.

PAMELA: Maybe you think you're a dork, but I think you're kinda cool.

MICHAEL: You do?

PAMELA: Yeah, you're so cool.

MICHAEL: I am?

PAMELA: Oh my god: Totally. And you know what? The thing about cool people—I mean, really cool people—is that they were all dorks when they were young. So...

MICHAEL: Thanks.

PAMELA: You know, this is really fun. Talking to you.

MICHAEL: Mom?

PAMELA: What?

MICHAEL: Can I ask you a question?

PAMELA: You're my son. I think that means you can ask me anything.

MICHAEL: I was wondering...can reptiles get cancer?

PAMELA: I don't know. Why?

MICHAEL: I was just thinking that maybe some of the dinosaurs got leukemia. And that's how some of them got extinct.

PAMELA: Maybe...

Beat.

...But they didn't have hospitals back then.

It's a good thing we have them now.

MICHAEL: Yeah.

PAMELA: I've spent a lot of time in this hospital. A lot of time. It never made me feel nervous before, but right now it's making me feel a little bit nervous. Do you feel nervous right now?

MICHAEL: A little bit.

PAMELA: You want me to tell you a story?

MICHAEL: Yeah.

PAMELA: I'm gonna need help because I'm not so good at this.

MICHAEL: Okay.

PAMELA: So.

Once upon a time there was a boy. And his name was...

MICHAEL: Michael?

PAMELA: Yes, his name was Michael.

MICHAEL: That's a good start.

PAMELA: And Michael was a really strong, beautiful, little boy...

Lights fade out.

END OF PLAY

About the Playwright

ERIK PATTERSON is an award-winning playwright, screenwriter, and writing teacher.

His play, *One of the Nice Ones*, earned the Los Angeles Drama Critics Circle Award. His theater work has been produced or developed by Playwrights' Arena, the Los Angeles Theatre Centre, Theatre of NOTE, the Evidence Room, The Actors' Gang, the Echo Theater Company, the Lark Play Development Center, Moving Arts, Black Dahlia, Naked Angels, the Mark Taper Forum, and New Group. His plays have been nominated for the Ovation Award, the Stage Raw Award, the LA Weekly Award, and the GLAAD Media Award.

His writing for TV has been recognized with the Humanitas Prize and the Writer's Guild Award, as well as two Emmy nominations. Along with his writing partner, Jessica Scott, Erik has written films for Warner Bros., Universal, 20th Century Fox, Disney, Freeform, MTV, Paramount, Hallmark, and Syfy, among others. Film and TV credits include: *Abandoned* (starring Emma Roberts and Michael Shannon), *R.L. Stine's The Haunting Hour*, *Another Cinderella Story* (starring Selena Gomez and Jane Lynch), *Deep Blue Sea 2*, *Radio Rebel*, and many more.

Erik is a graduate of Occidental College and the British American Drama Academy. He hosts a gently-guided writing sprint online called "Sunday Sprints" that attracts writers seeking community and inspiration to do their best work.

www.erikpatterson.org

Plays by Erik Patterson

Tonseisha
drama / 1 female, 5 male / 45 minutes, no intermission
A young Japanese woman is haunted by the loss of two men: her father, whom she barely knew, and cult novelist Richard Brautigan, whom she never met. Akiko plays out her father/Richard Brautigan fantasies with a new man nearly every night. Each one of her relationships begins in a bar and ends in a bedroom, and she's never satisfied. She's so lost...can she ever be found?

Yellow Flesh / Alabaster Rose
dark comedy / 5 female, 4 male / full length, one intermission
Elliot is lost in a world of sex workers—late night house calls from hustlers and phone calls with call girls. Becky is torn between two worlds—her day job as a stripper and being a mom to fifteen-year-old Rose (a Goth girl who wants nothing to do with her). And then there's Little B, who has stripped away every piece of herself until all she has left is her obsession with Icelandic pop singer Bjork. This troubled family's shared past holds unspeakable horrors and they must join forces if they ever want to heal. *Winner of the Backstage West Garland Award for Best Playwriting.*

Red Light, Green Light
drama / 6 female, 7 male / full length, one intermission
A gay clown. Two lesbian strippers. A pregnant Goth teen. A deadbeat dad. A horny mother. And a girl who thinks she's Bjork. In this stand-alone sequel to *Yellow Flesh / Alabaster Rose*, the Silverstein family journey towards healing is abruptly halted when Elliot becomes the victim of a brutal gay bashing.

He Asked For It
drama / 1 female, 6 male / full length, one intermission
It's the early 2000s, before PrEP. Ted is new to Los Angeles, and newly out of the closet. He goes on a journey through Hollywood back rooms, nightclub bathrooms, and Internet chat rooms—where he meets and falls in love with Henry. But Henry doesn't yet know how to navigate the dating landscape with his new HIV diagnosis, so he breaks things off with Ted...who then makes a desperate decision to win Henry back. *He Asked For It* asks how far are you willing to go for love? And how much will you forgive? *GLAAD Media Award nominee for Outstanding Los Angeles Theater.*

Sick
dramedy / 3 female, 3 male, 1 child / full length, no intermission
David needs to get laid, Gary could use a drink, and Tim would like you to take your top off. Carla craves cocaine, Jeannie's got God, and Pamela keeps digging herself deeper into the funny and frightening world of hypochondria. But when one of their own gets sick for real, they're all going to have to face their greatest fears and grow up.

I Wanna Hold Your Hand
dramedy / 3 female, 3 male / full length, no intermission
Our lives can change in an instant. One moment you're getting engaged, and a few surreal moments later you're sitting with strangers in an ICU waiting room, praying your fiancé will survive a brain aneurysm. While waiting for Frank to wake from a coma, Ada meets Julia, Paul, and Josh, who are waiting for their mom to wake up. A tenuous friendship is born. *I Wanna Hold Your Hand* looks at life, death, and recovery, and what it means to try your hand at living again...

One of the Nice Ones
dark comedy / 2 female, 2 male / 90 minutes, no intermission
A paraplegic woman plays outrageous power games to get something she desperately wants in this dark, twisty, sexy play that takes office politics to new extremes. *Winner of the Los Angeles Drama Critics Circle Award for Best Playwriting.*

Handjob
dark comedy / 2 female, 4 male / 90 minutes, no intermission
An encounter between a white, gay playwright and his black, straight "shirtless maid" goes disastrously wrong when signals are misinterpreted, lines crossed. *Handjob* explores the aftermath of their meeting, as it reveals deep layers of discrimination, discord, and discontent among people who should be allies. How do you know when you've gone too far if you completely ignore other people's boundaries?

Books by Erik Patterson

Pop Prompts: 200 Writing Prompts Inspired by Popular Music
Available in paperback and e-book

Pop Prompts is a collection of writing prompts that will help you dig deeper and break through creative blocks. Each prompt is paired with a pop song. Let the music be your muse as you work on your memoir, novel, script, poem—or even your own songs. This book can also be a daily jumpstart for therapeutic journaling. Use it however you want, whenever you want. As long as you're writing you're doing it right.

Pop Prompts For Swifties: 99 Writing Prompts
Available in paperback and e-book

Every writing prompt in this book is paired with one of Taylor's songs from the first "era" of her storytelling journey, from her debut album *Taylor Swift* (2006), to *Fearless* (2008), to *Speak Now* (2010), to *Red* (2012), and all the way through *1989* (2014). You don't even have to be a Swiftie—anyone can use these prompts for self-expression and reflection. As a bonus, each prompt includes blank journal pages. Inspiration is only a song away. Put on your favorite Taylor Swift album, pick a prompt, and start writing! Taylor Swift has no involvement in this book. The use of her name is merely descriptive and should not be interpreted as a sign of endorsement.

SUNDAY SPRINTS

Need some motivation?

Do you work better when someone is holding you accountable?

Come to SUNDAY SPRINTS.

Erik Patterson hosts gently-guided writing sprints on Zoom every Wednesday from 6 to 8 p.m. PST and every Sunday from noon to 2 p.m. PST. (Yes, it's called Sunday Sprints on Wednesdays because... why not?)

Here's how it works: I give a new writing prompt every fifteen minutes. You write. That's it.

All sprinters stay on mute. Alone but not alone, you can draw creative energy from the community of writers on your screen. This is a fun, low-pressure environment—a safe space for you to experiment with your writing. No worries: I will never ask you to share your work.

You decide how to use this distraction-free writing time. Work on that screenplay, novel, short story, play, poem, song. Do some therapeutic journaling. Write letters to loved ones. Do some technical writing. Create a D&D campaign. Finish your homework. Seriously, whatever you need to work on.

Let's get that writing done. Together.

Join the Sunday Sprints Patreon at:
www.patreon.com/erikpatterson

Subscribe to the Sunday Sprints mailing list at:
www.erikpatterson.org/sundaysprints

www.ingramcontent.com/pod-product-compliance
Lightning Source LLC
Chambersburg PA
CBHW072059110526
44590CB00018B/3243